Virtual Assistant Assistant:

The Ultimate Guide to Finding, Hiring, and Working with Virtual Assistants

Nick Loper

VirtualAssistantAssistant.com

Virtual Assistant Assistant: The Ultimate Guide to Finding, Hiring, and Working with Virtual Assistants

This book is intended for informational purposes only. You should consult with an attorney or CPA if you have any questions related to the tax and legal implications of working with virtual assistants.

Please understand there are some links contained in this book from which I may benefit financially.

The material in this book may include information, products, or services by third parties. These Third Party Materials consist of products and opinions expressed by their owners. As such, the author does not assume responsibility or liability for any Third Party material or opinions.

The publication of such Third Party Materials does not constitute the author's guarantee of any information, instruction, opinion, products, or services contained within the Third Party Material. The use of recommended Third Party Material does not guarantee any success and/or earnings related to you or your business. Publication of such Third Party Material is simply a recommendation and an expression of the author's own opinion of that material.

No part of this publication shall be reproduced, transmitted, or sold in whole or in part in any form, without the prior written consent of the author. All trademarks and registered trademarks appearing in this book are the property of their respective owners.

Users of this guide are advised to do their own due diligence when it comes to making business decisions and all information, products, and services that have been provided should be independently verified by your own qualified professionals. By reading this guide, you agree that the author is not responsible for the success or failure of your business decisions relating to any information presented in this book.

Is Outsourcing a Dirty Word?

The O word.

Let's talk about it.

In today's political discourse, few words have been demonized as much as outsourcing. Outsourcing has become the scapegoat for all our problems: from deficits and unemployment, to corporate greed and tax evasion. In his State of the Union address, President Obama even declared, *"No, we will not go back to an economy weakened by outsourcing."*

But is outsourcing really all that bad?

I mean, we all do it.

Last night, did you make dinner yourself or did you go out? Did you grow the food yourself? Did you wash the dishes by hand or did you put them in the dishwasher?

This year, did you do your taxes yourself, or did you hire an accountant? Was your accountant human, or did they take the form of software, like Turbo Tax?

Outsourcing is a fact of life. I need a computer for my work, but have no idea how to make one myself. So I outsourced that task to Dell. It was an easy decision.

Simply defined, outsourcing is a way to procure what you need **more effectively** than you could do it yourself.

How we determine what "effectively" means though, varies by each situation. In basic terms you can think of three factors to measure effectiveness:

1. Lower cost
2. Greater speed
3. Superior quality

For example, you probably could do your taxes yourself, but it will probably take you a long time and might not be as accurate as having them professionally done.

Outsourcing is about using resources efficiently. But while efficiency is universally praised, outsourcing remains vilified. Why?

Outsourcing has an image problem. The image that comes to mind is the American worker who lost his job to a lower-priced doppelganger in India. I don't mean to make light of this situation because it definitely does happen.

And no one is advocating sweat shops or abusive employee-employer relationships.

But what about the thousands of small business owners who outsource critical elements of their operation every day? These entrepreneurs are creating value not just in their own communities, but in communities around the world as well.

Say you have an idea for a killer new website, but don't know how to program a website. You could sit down and spend months or years learning html and php and web design, or you could hire someone who already has these skills. Your website gets built much faster and you start attracting customers sooner. In this way, **outsourcing *accelerates* value creation.**

The other misconception about outsourcing is that it's all overseas. You might be surprised to learn there is a thriving outsourcing economy right here in the United States. Look at the busy marketplaces like Upwork and you'll find thousands of talented local professionals ready to work.

Outsourcing doesn't have to be a dirty word. After all, anything that promotes efficiency, productivity, and value creation can't be so bad.

This book is about how to make outsourcing with virtual assistants work for you and your business. You'll learn how a virtual assistant can save you time, earn you more money, and help you live the life you want.

Let's get started.

TABLE OF CONTENTS

SECTION 1:

VIRTUAL ASSISTANT BASICS

What is a Virtual Assistant?

Simply put, a virtual assistant is someone who works for you remotely.

If you need help, either in the operations of business or just in your busy personal life, a virtual assistant can be a saving grace.

A virtual assistant can serve as a personal assistant, but thanks to our wired world, they no longer need to work from a desk right outside your office.

I have to admit, when I think of personal assistants, I used to have some glamorous and outdated vision of secretaries from decades ago like you might see in *Mad Men*. It's either that, or Smithers, Mr. Burns' right-hand man in *The Simpsons*.

Nowadays though, you don't need to be a high-powered executive or the richest man in town to have a personal assistant of your own. In fact, you can find qualified virtual assistants under $5 an hour if you know where to look.

The aim of this book is to show you:

- How a virtual assistant can save you time, money, and sanity
- How to hire the best talent for the best price
- How to work effectively with your VA to achieve your goals

The 3 Types of Virtual Assistants

Virtual assistants come in 3 types:

1. Task-based virtual assistants
2. Project-based virtual assistants
3. Virtual employees

1. Task-Based Virtual Assistants

Task-based virtual assistants specialize in **short, one-off tasks**. Normally these are mini-projects, like appointment setting or online research, that you could take care of yourself, but instead choose to outsource them for the time-saving benefits.

Examples of possible tasks:

- Find three pet-friendly hotels in Austin, TX, and send me a link to their Trip Advisor pages
- Get car insurance quotes
- Pick 3 Napa wineries and make tasting reservations for Saturday for 6 people

Task-based assistance is usually **sold as a monthly package** that includes a set number of requests. There is a pool of VAs available, and each handles different tasks from different customers as they come in.

Starting at just $25 per month, this is the cheapest form of outsourcing available.

In most cases, you won't have a dedicated point-of-contact, which can be a downside depending on the kind of jobs you might need done. Some task-based VA companies do offer dedicated support for a premium price-point.

Still, it can be **a great way to practice delegating** and get your feet wet with a virtual assistant for a minimal investment and commitment.

Leading Task-Based Virtual Assistant Companies:

- *OkayRelax* (*Philippines*) – $20 for 5 tasks per month.
- *Fancy Hands (USA)* – Starts at $30/mo. for 5 tasks.
- *Efficise (Pakistan)* – $45 for 30 tasks per month.

2. Project-Based Virtual Assistants

A project-based virtual assistant is a **freelance contractor** who helps you with a one-time project, and nothing else.

Perhaps you need a website designed, some articles written, or an iPhone app programmed. If you can't (or don't want to) do these things yourself, a virtual assistant is the way to go.

The best resources for finding freelance virtual assistants are the global marketplaces of Upwork.com, Freelancer.com, PeoplePerHour.com, and others. These sites allow you to post your exact requirements for free, receive bids from qualified workers around the world, and choose which one you like best.

For project-based VAs, I've spent as little as $5 and as much as $10,000 and beyond. It all depends on the size and scope of the project. Obviously, the bigger the project and the more money that is at stake, the more carefully I'll review the candidates.

The ecosystems of the various freelance sites mentioned are a good place to start for portfolio samples and reviews, but I would recommend going outside the walls of that site as well. See if you can find this person or company on Google, LinkedIn, Facebook, or Twitter. What are other people saying about them?

If your project has business-sensitive material, you can request the freelancers sign a non-disclosure agreement before they get all the details. Most won't hesitate, and it's crucial they know all the expectations and specifications upfront so they can provide an accurate bid.

Finally, if you're spending significant money, don't initiate the project without an interview. Actually speaking to your freelance virtual assistant can make a huge difference and help uncover any potential language barriers and misunderstandings down the road.

3. Virtual Employees

The primary focus of this book will be on the third type of virtual assistants: **virtual employees**. Virtual employees are part-time or full-time workers that help you in your business, just as an in-house employee would. The only difference is they do it remotely.

A virtual employee is a single, dedicated resource for your business. This is a person you will train and **work closely with on an ongoing basis**.

It's the best of both worlds; this type of virtual assistant can handle the work of both the task-based VA and the project-based VA, in addition to your business process outsourcing.

With a virtual employee, you can negotiate whatever working hours fit your needs and your budget. Many VAs prefer to work full-time for a single employer, while others are perfectly content balancing multiple bosses at once. In that case, their work never gets boring if they are reporting to 4 different clients, all contracting for 10-hours a week!

The rates for a virtual employee will vary from less than $5/hr all the way up to $40/hr or more depending on their geographic location, experience, and areas of expertise. In some parts of the world, you can get a full-time VA for as little as $500 per month.

I prefer to work with virtual employees because I believe it is **the most effective outsourcing method** over the long-term.

Why Hire a Virtual Assistant?

A virtual assistant can help you regain control of your life at a sometimes surprisingly low cost. When we think of personal assistants we might think of high-powered CEOs and A-list celebrities, but 21st Century technology has brought the personal assistant within reach of almost everyone. Because of our wired global society and low telecommunications costs, a virtual assistant can work for you from just about any corner of the world.

But what can a virtual assistant do for you? Nearly anything that doesn't require a physical presence. Virtual assistants can accomplish an amazing variety of tasks including:

- Scheduling appointments and responding to phone calls or emails
- Online research and travel arrangements
- Accounting and bookkeeping
- Article writing and online marketing
- Event planning
- Customer service

- Or just about anything else you can think of

If a virtual assistant can save you even just an hour a day, wouldn't that be worthwhile? Yes, it will cost you a few dollars, but you have to consider what your time is worth. An extra hour to spend working on truly **meaningful projects** or with friends or family can yield a priceless return.

A virtual assistant will free up your time to focus on sales or higher-level strategic business activities. For example, you may be bogged down with low-value administrative tasks that take away from your high-value work.

At its most basic, work can be broken down into **activities that make you money**, and those that don't. Why spend time on those that don't?

You can train your virtual assistant to do whatever task you need done. This is especially valuable if you have certain simple, repetitive tasks that take up a lot of your time.

I've met too many entrepreneurs who are stuck working in their business instead of on it; a virtual assistant could be their ticket to growing profits and **personal freedom**.

Take Control by Letting Go

This is my story. Does it sound familiar?

My first experience in hiring a virtual assistant was when I had an idea for a website. If I wanted to turn my idea into reality, I had a couple options:

1. I could learn how to build the website myself.
2. I could hire someone who already knew how to build it.

Since I was busy working full-time already, I decided it would be a more efficient use of resources to hire someone else. Using Guru.com I met a web developer who became my first "virtual assistant." That was in 2005 and we're still working together today!

A few months later, the website launched and continued to grow each year. I was very excited to see my little side project turning into a viable business.

In 2008 I decided to quit my job and focus on the business full time. It was totally rewarding and I was feeling **the rush of entrepreneurship**. Unfortunately it was also taking up all my time.

I knew I needed help but wasn't sure what do to. That's the problem with being your own boss; there's no one else around to make the tough decisions for you.

Like many small business owners, **I had trust issues** over letting someone new into my operation and "trade secrets." I thought whoever I hired would do poor quality work - or worse - copy my idea!

The other issue? I was scared of the time it might take to hire, interview, and train a brand new employee in my systems. Sure it might save me time and headache in the long-run, but in the short-run I've got work to do!

This is known as being "**too busy chopping down trees to sharpen the saw**."

Well, after a particularly brutal month, I reached my pain threshold and overcame my fears. I finally took the time to "sharpen the saw" and haven't looked back since.

With my newfound free time I was able to zoom-out and focus on some bigger picture projects I had been neglecting. On top of that, I was able to leverage the expertise of my VA to generate new business ideas and tactics I had never even thought of.

Every entrepreneur reaches a ceiling, the natural limit of what they can accomplish on their own. If you're happy working up to that ceiling, that's totally OK.

But my guess is if you're reading this, you want to bust through that ceiling and achieve even more business, financial, and personal growth.

Virtual Assistant Benefits

The way I see it, there are three main benefits to hiring a virtual assistant.

Save time

The reason most people start looking for a virtual assistant is because they are simply too busy, and they know a virtual assistant can save them time. By offloading your routine time-consuming tasks, a virtual assistant can literally **add hours to your day**.

Imagine using those hours to meet new clients and explore new business opportunities, catch up with friends, or spend more time with your family. Time is our **most valuable resource**, and the one we end up wasting more often than anything else.

Save money

Virtual assistants can save you money in a couple ways. First, if you are already considering hiring an in-house employee, a virtual assistant is **a much cheaper alternative**.

They can also help save you money in the tasks they perform, whether it be researching online deals or improving the **return on investment** of your business's marketing efforts.

Save headache

To many customers, a virtual assistant is **peace of mind**. You have someone on call to help deal with whatever life throws at you.

Plus, when you use a virtual assistant company, you don't have to worry about things like payroll processing, employment taxes, fair hiring and firing regulations, providing equipment and office space, and other stress-inducing problems.

How Much is Your Time Worth?

Do you know your effective hourly wage? Although this calculation has become somewhat clichéd in recent years, it's still important to understand what an hour of work should be worth to us.

If you work a standard 40-hour week and make $50,000 a year, what is your effective hourly wage?

Well, take 40 hours a week multiplied by 52 weeks in a year and you end up with 2,080 working hours. $50,000 divided by 2,080 hours is roughly $24 an hour.

If you make $100,000 and still work only 40 hours a week, your rate is $48 an hour.

Now you can see where hiring a VA at $5 or $10 an hour starts to make a lot of sense.

Use the worksheet below to calculate your own effective hourly wage:

Annual Income	$ _____	
Hours per Week	_____	Hours
Work Weeks per Year	_____	Weeks
(hey, maybe you only work 9 months a year)		
Total Work Hours	_____	Total Hours
(multiply hours x weeks)		
Effective Hourly Wage	$ _____	
(divide Annual Income by Total Hours)		

Lawyers, accountants, architects, and other professionals tend to think in terms of "billable hours." Billable hours are time spent directly on revenue-generating work.

I think a billable hours mindset can be applicable to nearly everyone. **Focus on what rings the cash register and delegate the rest**.

What's Your Excuse?

As mentioned previously, I had some doubts and hesitations before I was ready to hire a virtual assistant. Sometimes these excuses can become paralyzing, so I thought it would be important to address the three most common ones in more detail.

At various times I've been guilty of all of these:

1. I Can't Trust a VA

Many solo entrepreneurs, myself included, are so used to doing *everything* themselves, they find it hard to delegate *anything*.

I was afraid my virtual assistant would do poor quality work that might end up hurting my business. Or worse yet, I feared they might even try to steal my ideas. The more people I talked to, the more I found this to be a really common fear.

Indeed, it can be scary to open the doors of your business to someone new (and potentially someone half-way around the world).

However, if you never overcome it, you're stuck doing everything yourself. I hate to say it, but **you don't have a business; you have a job**. What if Steve Jobs or Bill Gates had never hired any help?

The quality of work issue can be overcome by hiring a talented VA, giving them specific guidelines and expectations, and training them in your systems.

And the concern that your VA might steal your ideas? I've been working with VAs since 2005, and have never once had this be an issue. I'm sure it's happened somewhere in the world but I can't imagine it being a serious problem. If that's all that's holding you back, ask your VA to sign a non-disclosure/non-compete agreement.

2. I Can Do it Better or Faster Myself

If you've been doing a certain task for years, it's probably second nature by now. And I don't doubt it that you can do it better or faster than nearly anyone else. You shouldn't necessarily expect your VA to outperform you right out of the gate – instead you should ask, "What would be the best use of my time?"

If you're spending hours each day on tasks that could be delegated to a virtual assistant, I'm almost positive you could use those hours more effectively to grow your business, close more deals, strategize for the future, or just spend more time with your family.

3. I'll Lose Too Much Time Training Them

We'll take a closer look at training later in this book, but the training time requires a long-term mindset. It's true you'll need to make a time investment in training at the onset of your virtual assistant relationship. However, that investment can generate exponential returns by freeing up hours of your work schedule for weeks, months, or even years to come.

So what's your excuse?

What a Virtual Assistant Can Do for You

Aside from fetching your coffee and picking up the dry cleaning (although now there are *local* VA companies that facilitate these kinds of tasks), there's really no limit to the kinds of jobs a virtual assistant can do for you.

Here is the unofficial giant list to get your juices flowing:

1.   Add images to your presentations or blog posts

2.   Answer phone calls

3.   Archive old files

4.   Audit your bills

5.   Backup your data

6.   Brainstorm new business opportunities

7.   Brainstorm topics for new blog articles

8.   Build backlinks to your site

9.   Build spreadsheets

10. Check your other VA's work

11. Check your website for broken links

12. Compile mailing lists

13. Compile motivational quotes

14. Conduct keyword research

15. Conduct market research

16. Coordinate conference calls

17. Coordinate meetings and appointments

18. Create a "keep in touch" schedule for people you don't see often

19. Create a budget

20. Create a database

21. Create a diet plan

22. Create a list of forums relevant to your business

23. Create a marketing plan

24. Create a meal plan

25. Create a playlist

26. Create a project tracking system

27. Create a Squidoo lens

28. Create a time tracking system

29. Create an email newsletter

30. Create an exercise plan

31. Create and conduct a client survey

32. Create and format charts from your reports

33. Create and maintain a list of press releases

34. Create and send welcome package to new clients

35. Create business process documentation

36. Create financial projections for your business

37. Create flyers

38. Create labels

39. Create presentations

40. Data clean-up

41. Data entry

42. Design a webpage

43. Design brochures

44. Design business cards

45. Distribute press releases

46. Do A/B testing on your website or marketing efforts

47. Do fact checking

48. Do user testing

49. Do your taxes

50. Draft a cover letter

51. Edit blog posts

52. Edit photos

53. Edit sales letters

54. Edit websites

55. Enter contacts into Outlook

56. File documents

57. Fill out routine paperwork

58. Filter the news

59. Filter your email

60. Find a plumber

61. Find an apartment or house when you move

62. Find contact information for others in your niche

63. Find new clients

64. Find the lowest airfare

65. Fix broken links on your website

66. Follow up on business leads

67. Fulfill product orders

68. Help set up a website or blog

69. Help with a job search

70. Help with homework

71. Install WordPress and popular plug-ins

72. Interface design

73. Keep you accountable

74. Make announcements via Twitter or Facebook

75. Make bank deposits

76. Make follow-up calls

77. Manage direct mail campaigns

78. Manage guest lists

79. Manage social media accounts

80. Manage your affiliate program

81. Manage your calendar

82. Manage your live chat customer service

83. Manage your voicemail

84. Merge files

85. Moderate blog comments

86. Moderate forum posts

87. Monitor cash flow

88. Monitor Quora and Yahoo Answers for questions you could answer

89. Monitor Twitter for company or client mentions

90. Monitor your Google Alerts

91. Motivate you

92. Online shopping

93. Optimize AdWords campaigns

94. Optimize Facebook ad campaigns

95. Order promotional items

96. Order supplies

97. Organize files

98. Organize your inbox

99. Pay bills

100. Perform online research

101. Place online advertisements

102. Plan a party

103. Plan a trip

104. Plan a wedding

105. Plan an event

106. Post ads to Craigslist or other classified sites

107. Prepare and send 1099s to contractors

108. Prepare and ship pre-meeting materials

109. Prepare financial reports

110. Prepare meeting materials

111. Proofread your documents

112. Provide live customer phone support

113. Purge files

114. Recommend a dentist

115. Recruit and screen employees or other VAs

116. Research best practices in your industry

117. Research conference room & meeting space rentals

118. Research contractors

119. Research hotels and resorts

120. Research products

121. Research schools

122. Research the important facts of any industry

123. Research vendors

124. Respond to blog / Facebook comments

125. Respond to customer support emails

126. Return phone calls

127. Run eBay auctions

128. Run errands

129. Run reports

130. Scan business cards and enter into contacts

131. Scan documents

132. Scan pictures

133. Screen phone calls

134. Send birthday / anniversary cards to clients

135. Send direct mail pieces

136. Send email newsletters

137. Send flowers to your wife

138. Send follow-up emails

139. Send holiday cards

140. Send invitations

141. Send invoices to clients

142. Send reminders

143. Send thank you gifts

144. Send you daily reports

145. Set up an email auto-responder series

146. Set up an email list

147. Set up local lunch meetings with potential partners and mentors

148. Submit articles to directories

149. Submit press releases

150. Syndicate videos online

151. Teach you something new

152. Track customer responses

153. Track event attendees

154. Track inventory levels

155. Train other VAs

156. Transcribe meetings

157. Transcribe podcasts

158. Transcribe voice memos

159. Update files

160. Update your website

161. Upload ebooks to Amazon

162. Upload photos to Facebook

163. Upload photos to Flickr

164. Upload podcasts to iTunes

165. Welcome new clients

166. Write a grant application

167. Write blog posts

168. Write thank you notes

Should You Outsource Social Media?

There's no doubt that to "do" social media right, it takes a lot of time and energy. Because of this, social media management is one service nearly every virtual assistant company offers.

The question is: is social media something you should be outsourcing?

The Case Against

Think of the primary rules of social media engagement — be yourself, listen, be authentic, and most importantly, **care**. Will any outsourced social media manager care as much as you?

For personal brands, I think hiring someone to run 100% of your social media presence is risky. After all, your brand is about YOU, and the various social media platforms give people an honest chance to **connect with the real you**. If they find out someone else is calling the shots it could hurt your brand and your reputation, and ultimately your bottom line.

Yes, it can be time-consuming to reply to twitter comments, but it's not that time-consuming. Will a virtual assistant be able to portray your brand the way you want it?

I would be especially hesitant having an overseas VA handle your social media accounts. The reason being is they will probably have different social norms than your audience. What may be perfectly acceptable in terms of language and response time in India might not play so well in the US.

Often this kind of cultural disconnect is relatively harmless, but sometimes it can be downright offensive. In the wake of the July 2012 Aurora, Colorado movie theater shooting, "Aurora" was understandably a trending topic on twitter. Unfortunately CelebBoutique.com's outsourced social media team hadn't heard the news when they tweeted this gem:

> "#Aurora is trending, clearly about our Kim K inspired #Aurora dress ;) Shop [link]..."

Ouch.

The Case For

You can't do everything yourself. Well you can, but only up to a certain point. Once you reach that ceiling you're going to have to get some help if you want to **keep growing**.

Companies are still taking care of their customers and maintaining a valuable social media presence, even though the founder isn't personally posting every day.

At least I assume Richard Branson isn't managing the @VirginAmerica account!

It's naive to think a virtual assistant couldn't do as good (or better) a job managing your online profiles. Especially if they have more experience with the various networks and tools.

I'm confident you can find a VA that will be a great steward for your brand online. They might charge more than $5 an hour, but that's the price you have to pay to stay active and engaged in social media, while **protecting and promoting your brand**.

And by outsourcing social media, it will force you into a more managerial role.

How Much Does a VA Cost?

I've already touched a little on how affordable a virtual assistant can be, but let's take a closer look at the costs.

At the lower end of the market (in the Philippines for example), you may find a **full-time VA for less than $500 a month**. It seems crazy, right? Surprisingly, this is actually a strong wage in their local economy and allows them the freedom and flexibility to work-from-home.

If you prefer your VA to work in an office environment, the rates will be a little higher due to the increased overhead. Still, you can get an overseas virtual assistant in the $1000 per month range by going through a virtual assistant company.

In the US and other developed economies, home-based VAs can range anywhere from $10-50 per hour, and virtual assistant companies charge **$2000 or more**, and that will still be for part-time help.

So **there's no definitive answer as to how much a VA costs**.

The truth is, it depends. The three biggest factors affecting the cost are:

1. **Geographic location** – The lower the cost of living, the less income your VA needs to bring in.
2. **Skills** – In-demand skills like software development and programming will command higher rates than less specialized skills, such as general administrative tasks.
3. **Overhead** – Generally, home-based freelance virtual assistants are going to be cheaper than their office-dwelling counterparts.

Perhaps the more important question to ask is, how much *less* does a VA cost than hiring someone in-house?

Virtual Assistants vs. In-House Employees

Cost Comparison

A virtual assistant is significantly less expensive than hiring an in-house employee.

For the calculations below, I used the rates listed on the previous page for the overseas VAs, and used a low-end wage of $15/hr for the US freelancers.

	Filipino Freelancer		Overseas VA Company		US Freelancer		In-House Employee	
Monthly Salary	$	500	$	1,000	$	2,400	$	2,400
Employer Taxes*							$	184
Benefits**							$	1,008
Total Monthly Cost	$	500	$	1,000	$	2,400	$	3,592
Total Annual Cost	$	6,000	$	12,000	$	28,800	$	43,099

*Calculated at 6.2% for Social Security and 1.45% for Medicare.

**Calculated at 42%, the 2012 national average according to the Bureau of Labor Statistics.

Source: http://www.bls.gov/ro9/ececwest.htm

As you can see, your business can realize **massive savings** by hiring a virtual assistant over hiring someone in-house. Think of what you could do with an extra $30,000 a year!

Other Burdens

These figures don't take into consideration some other crucial aspects of hiring a local employee.

For example, **where are they going to work**? I work from home and don't have any extra office space for an in-house assistant.

On top of that, a virtual assistant provides their own workstation. With a new local employee, you may have to **buy them a computer** and software to work on.

Plus, virtual assistants help you save on overhead and other **regulatory headaches**. Not that you would treat any employee unfairly, but there are a whole mess of fair hiring and firing laws you would have to become familiar with to bring someone on board locally.

Keep in mind you will also incur additional time and accounting expense in **processing payroll** and other government files. When it comes to paperwork, my preference is always to do less of it.

No matter how you slice it, virtual assistants offer significant cost savings over traditional employees.

What About Security?

Security is a major concern when working with virtual assistants, especially when it comes to sensitive business files, account access, and personal financial data like credit cards.

Sensitive Files

All outsourcing companies have security measures in place to prevent unauthorized access to your files. Those with modern office infrastructure will be happy to tell you about their SSL encrypting technology, redundant backups, and strict data privacy policy.

Some will go so far as to restrict employees from bringing external storage devices like USB memory sticks onto the premises.

But despite the best protections, it's simply not possible to prevent every potential security breach. In the example above, what's to stop a virtual employee from emailing sensitive files to an external account?

We run the same risks in hiring locally, as one bad individual can cause a security headache whether they're down the hall or on the other side of the world.

In working with home-based virtual assistants, the only security measure you have is the person's **integrity**. You can have them sign a privacy document, which may or may not be enforceable in their location, but there has to be a certain amount of **trust** for the relationship to work.

Thankfully I've never had any issues with data security with either office-based VAs or home-based VAs.

Granted, I'm not working on anything that would be a national security risk if it got leaked, but there certainly have been some proprietary documents, business secrets, software code, and process tutorials that I'm definitely happy *weren't* stolen or accessed by my competitors.

Account Access

I don't like giving out my passwords. It just feels like a bad idea, even when you trust the recipient.

One of the best workarounds I've found is a free tool called LastPass. It allows your virtual assistant to access certain accounts you set up for them, without them seeing your passwords.

Then, if things aren't going well, you can kill their LastPass profile and immediately lock them out of all your accounts.

Side note: LastPass is an amazing piece of software even if you're not using it to securely share account access with a virtual assistant. It saves me a ton of time and brain capacity in not having to remember dozens of different logins.

Credit Cards

If you find appealing the idea of having a virtual assistant book travel for you or make other purchases on your behalf, you may be wondering how this is technically accomplished without compromising your credit card information.

I reached out to several virtual assistant companies to ask how they handled credit card security for their clients.

With freelance and stay-at-home VAs, there is usually no secure online system to input your credit card information. Instead, you just call your VA and read them the card information over the phone, and they keep it in a safe place.

"It is a trust thing," Patty Grace of eaHELP explains. Her company is a virtual staffing agency based in Atlanta, Georgia. All the assistants work from their own home offices. Beyond trust, eaHELP has all their VAs sign privacy/confidentiality agreements to protect this kind of sensitive client data.

Other virtual assistant companies give you the option to store your credit card information in their secured system. Since they likely already had to invest in the online security measures for their own sign-up checkout process, it's not a huge leap to store the data for use by their VAs.

With the overseas companies, it's more common for only the shift managers (more tenured employees) to have access to client credit card data.

Red Butler, the Southern California virtual concierge service, will make purchases on your behalf from stores where you have a pre-existing account and a stored card. For other transactions, a dedicated representative will call you to get the credit card information in real time and complete the order.

A more elegant solution is offered by Fancy Hands, the New York-based virtual assistant company. Their VAs can make online purchases for you using a company credit card, and then just bill the card you have on file with them for the total amount, plus a $0.99 transaction fee. This service is currently limited to $200 (not a good option for expensive plane tickets!) but I tested it myself on an Amazon order and it worked well.

In addition, an important thing to remember is that most credit cards come with zero-liability fraud protection, meaning if for whatever reason your card becomes compromised and unauthorized purchases are made, you won't be on the hook for the bill. Of course it's best to never have to use that feature, but it's nice to know it's there.

Legal Implications

Disclaimer

I definitely need to start this section out by saying I'm not a lawyer, nor do I play one on TV. What follows is my general understanding of the rules, and you should probably take the time to find out what applies to your situation (or have your VA do it!).

Is it Legal to Hire Someone Overseas?

Absolutely. If you work with a freelancer, they are considered just an **independent contractor** to your company. If you work through a virtual assistant company overseas, that doesn't set you up for any new legal or tax liabilities in their home country or yours.

What About Taxes?

One of the beautiful things of working with virtual assistants is avoiding the **federal payroll taxes.** Your VA may still be liable for income taxes, but it is not your responsibility to withhold earnings.

Certain VA companies may charge a sales tax on top of their service fee, but this is rare.

1099s

As you know, you are required to provide a form 1099 to contractors with whom you spend over $600 in the calendar year, and send a copy to the IRS. However, if your virtual assistant is outside the US, there is **no need to provide the 1099** because the IRS isn't going to tax them anyway.

If your VA or VA company is based in the US, **a 1099 is required**. However, if you find your virtual assistant through one of the major freelance marketplaces (Upwork, etc.), they will automatically take care of this requirement for you.

And as someone who has filed several 1099s, I can say it's **a very simple process** and not one you should worry about. It only takes a few minutes and it's important to remember it's an information-only return – no tax is due from you; it just lets the IRS know your virtual assistant earned some money from you, and that the IRS should expect to get tax *from them*.

Write-Offs

Your virtual assistant is a **legitimate business expense**, no matter where they are located in the world. Because of that, you can **deduct their wages** from your corporate income.

Benefits

Since your virtual assistant is a contractor, you are not required to pay for benefits such as health care or pension plans. If they are an employee of a virtual assistant company, the company may already be providing these benefits. If they are a freelancer, they are on their own.

That said, if you have a virtual assistant you absolutely love and want to work with long-term, thinking about providing benefits would be a great idea.

It could be something as simple as paid vacation or sick days, or a monthly stipend to cover insurance premiums. These are the little things that can help make your VA a loyal partner in your business.

What Does the Affordable Care Act Mean for Small Businesses?

President Obama's health care reform package creates some new considerations for small businesses evaluating what benefits they offer their employees.

Small businesses that provide health insurance for their workers earn a **tax credit**.

Companies with less than 25 employees that provide health insurance can qualify for an immediate tax credit of up to 50% of their insurance costs, and of course the remainder of the insurance costs can be deducted from the company's taxable income as a business expense.

This tax credit provision is an **incentive for small businesses to provide insurance**, and applies only to companies where the average employee earns less than $50,000 per year.

On the flip side, companies with 50 or more employees actually **face a tax penalty** if they choose not to provide insurance. The penalty is $2000 per year for every full-time employee, minus the first 30 workers.

For example: a 75-person company that doesn't provide health insurance would be hit with a $90,000 fine. ($2000 x (75-30) = $90,000)

So what does all this have to do with virtual assistants?

For growing small businesses near the 50-person threshold, that can't afford to provide insurance, **a virtual assistant is a natural alternative** to paying the fine. Obviously this isn't the intent of the law, but the cause-and-effect is inevitable.

Myth: Virtual Assistants are a Third-World Industry

With all the excitement over *The 4-Hour Work Week* and advertisements for dirt-cheap VAs overseas, it's easy to overlook the fact that there is a thriving virtual assistant industry in the US and other developed countries.

In fact, VAnetworking.com, a social network and forum for virtual assistants boasts more than 28,000 members. Of these, more than 95% are from the US, Canada, Europe, and Australia.

The site got its start in 2003, well before personal outsourcing went mainstream. Founder Tawnya Sutherland, a single mother of three at the time, knew there was an army of work-from-home VAs out there who could use an online community of their own.

The vast majority of virtual assistants are women, and most started their VA business later in life. Indeed, what better opportunity to work flexible hours from home and use your existing skills to create value for clients?

And these are not $5/hour workers.

- 88% charge $20/hour or more for their services.
- 58% charge $30/hour or more.

As you can see, there is a strong market for skilled virtual assistants even at the higher price points.

Potential employers can submit a request for proposal at VAnetworking.com/clients to reach thousands of freelance VAs.

Virtual Assistant Certifications

Anyone with Internet access can open a virtual assistant business simply by declaring, *"I'm a virtual assistant!"* With so few barriers to entry, you may be wondering if there are any certifications, industry associations, or third-party guidelines that VAs must meet.

The **International Virtual Assistants Association** is a non-profit trade association for the virtual assistant industry. The IVAA supports the global VA community in a number of ways, including offering certification.

Their Certified Virtual Assistant program is open to members only, and is designed to be a badge of professionalism and to set VAs apart from the competition when trying to land clients. IVAA membership is $14.99 per month or $137 when paid annually.

The CVA program consists of 5 skills tests and costs an additional $150.

VAnetworking.com offers a certification program called VA Certified.

The review process considers a VAs professional work experience, their education and training, their "contributions to the VA industry," and of course, their ability to pay the $95 application fee. No tests are involved.

The Bottom Line?

While these certifications definitely show potential clients that a VA is serious about their business – and I would hold the IVAA certification in higher esteem than the VA Certified badge – **I wouldn't hesitate to consider "uncertified" VAs as well**.

My Current Virtual Assistant "Stack"

This is my current outsourcing set-up (updated 2016*).

Non-Dedicated Assistants

GoButler

GoButler (gobutlernow.com) is a **free** text-message based assistant service.

I use them for research tasks (i.e. "what am I allowed to bring into Wrigley Field food-wise?"), appointment setting ("make a service appointment for my wife's car"), and even some shopping stuff ("I saw these jeans at Nordstrom; anyone have them on sale?").

How can they afford to offer this service for free? I'm not even sure, but my speculation is they'll earn affiliate commission on monetizable requests, like if I had ended up purchasing those jeans through their system.

Fancy Hands

Fancy Hands (fancyhands.com) is a US-based task assistance service starting at $30/mo. I've been a Fancy

Hands member for years, and have used them for help with research, data entry, proofreading, and lots more.

Primarily what they do for me today is respond to the virtual assistant survey submissions on VirtualAssistantAssistant.com. Based on the responses, I have several templates of suggestions, and the cool thing is it's all automated and on average they reply much faster than I used to when I was (ironically) doing it all myself.

Dedicated Assistants

MyTasker

MyTasker (mytasker.com) is a helpful India-based VA company I've been working with regularly for the last year or so.

My dedicated assistant Bhaskar handles a couple recurring daily tasks for me, including drafting some client emails and saving them in my drafts folder in Gmail.

I've found the service super-reliable and a big time-saver. Rates start at $120/month.

OkayRelax

OkayRelax (okayrelax.com) is kind a hybrid model between a task-based, team-based service like Fancy Hands and a fully dedicated assistant.

You still get a bucket of tasks to submit each month (25 tasks for $75), but you're assigned a single dedicated assistant. That means turnaround times may be slower than with a pooled service, but hopefully you can realize the advantages of a dedicated assistant like trust in your business, some specialized training, and more consistent quality performance.

Right now I'm having my assistant John focus on research and data entry tasks, but am looking forward to expanding our relationship this year.

Specialist Freelancers

Rounding out my outsourcing "stack" are a handful of on-demand contractors.

The person I turn to most consistently is a writer who helps me out with website articles and podcast notes. But in the past few months I've also turned to specialists for social media graphic help and of course technical web development support.

Finally, I hired a podcast editing service to help clean up the audio for my weekly podcast, The Side Hustle Show.

I connected with my writer and graphic "guys" through my network and social media, and with my most recent web development project guy through the Codeable.io marketplace.

*Later in the book, I'll reference a virtual employee hired through Elance.com. I worked with a couple similarly-sourced assistants for several years before my business needs changed. When the time comes, I'll use the same strategies to find a new hire.

SECTION 2:

HOW TO HIRE A VIRTUAL ASSISTANT

Know Thyself

Let me give you a quick background. I was overwhelmed with work and was getting burned out with the day-to-day operation of the business. This was a bad sign because I normally

loved my work and hated the fact it was starting to control my life (and not the other way around).

I knew I needed help, but the thought of hiring someone was too stressful. Where would they work? What would my tax and payroll filing requirements be? Would I have to provide equipment? Or benefits?

It was at about that time I discovered virtual assistants, and it felt like a whole new world had opened up to me. I could get the help I needed, without the administrative headaches of a local employee. Although there will always be bumps in the road (I'll try and help you avoid them!), a VA was a perfect solution for me, and I think it can be for you too.

Like most solopreneurs, **the biggest challenge was letting go**. I had this fear that if I hired a VA to help me, they were eventually going to steal my ideas and put me out of business. Completely unfounded and unrealistic? Yes. But it was something I was afraid of.

I've since realized that competitors will always be there, and that your VA isn't going to be one of them. (They have a different mindset, but if you're still worried about it, ask them to sign a non-compete agreement.)

I was also afraid they wouldn't do a good job and screw things up. And it's true; they probably won't be as good as you at certain tasks. But I'm positive you can find some time-consuming projects a virtual assistant can get done with a similar or even greater level of proficiency.

The first secret to successfully working with a virtual assistant is to **know yourself**. Specifically:

- What are you good at?
- What are you not-so-good at?
- What do you enjoy doing?
- What tasks drive you crazy?
- What do you need to do to grow your business?
- What would you do if you only had more time?

Take the time to answer these questions. Understanding your own strengths and weaknesses is an important step before you hire a VA. I would create a list:

Love: Writing content, talking to clients, making videos

Hate: Accounting, database maintenance, research

Your answers will probably look a little different from mine, but you should really write them down because you're going to use them right away.

Know Your Requirements

Now that you've analyzed what you like to do, what you're good at, and what you need to do, it's time to figure out how to unload everything else. I mean why spend your precious time doing the stuff you hate and are terrible at?

For me it was valuable to spend a week tracking how I spent my time. I wrote down each activity and the amount of time I spent on it. Try it for a day; you might be surprised with the results.

Here's a sample list:

Read and respond to personal email – 45 minutes

Read and respond to customer email – 1 hour

Research for blog post – 1 hour

Write blog post – 1 hour

Update Twitter and Facebook – 5 minutes ... and then it turned into 30 minutes...

Go to the gym – 1 hour

Design new ad banner – 30 minutes

Daily website maintenance – 1.5 hours

Keyword research – 30 minutes

Phone call with prospective client – 45 minutes

Bookkeeping – 15 minutes

The next step is to determine which of these tasks you can outsource. In the most extreme cases, I've seen people outsource everything on this list aside from going to the gym. (And I'm sure some people wish they could outsource that too!)

It might be tempting to try and go big and aim for the promised land of the 4-Hour Work Week right out of the gate, but I would caution against that. It's all about baby steps. If this is going to be your first time working with a VA, let's start small.

From that list, choose a handful of tasks you'd like your VA to get off your plate. For example, maybe you start with:

Blog research – 1 hour

Blog writing – 1 hour

Daily website maintenance – 1.5 hours

Keyword research – 30 minutes

Now that you have a general idea of what your VA will be doing and how much time it should take them, it's also a good time to start thinking about your other requirements:

- Does your VA need to be at work at the same time you are?
- Do they need to be a native English speaker?
- Are there specific skills they should already have, or will you provide training?
- What is your budget?

Next up, we'll examine how to turn your requirements into an attention-getting job listing.

A Word on Budget: How Much Should You Pay a VA?

The virtual assistant industry is a diverse and growing marketplace of companies and freelancers, and because of this, you will find a huge spectrum of prices. In general, the old rule of **"you get what you pay for"** still applies, but that's not to say there aren't any high-value bargain-basement VAs out there.

Despite what some other websites will tell you, you're unlikely to find quality workers for $3 an hour in any part of the world. That said, do you need to pay some professional $40 an hour to get good results? Probably not.

My advice: **Pay a fair wage** and move on. Overseas that will be between $5 and $10 an hour; in the US, it can be $15 to $25 an hour or more.

One age-old business rule that definitely applies is to simply **hire the best talent you can afford**.

If you underpay your VA, how motivated are they going to be to go the extra mile and really help you?

If your business-model allows for it, you might also consider an incentive plan to reward strong performance. For example, if your VA is helping customers on your website via live chat, why not give him or her a piece of each sale they help close? This is what I do and it's been working out really well.

The 2 Types of Delegation (One is WAY Harder to Pull Off)

When you're looking at your list of potential tasks to delegate or outsource, you'll find that the items fall into one of two categories:

1. Stuff you know how to do, but your time would be better spent elsewhere.

2. Stuff you don't know how to do, but needs to get done.

Earlier I told you about my current virtual assistant "stack." Nearly everything on that list fell into **the first category**: stuff I know how to do and very easily could do myself.

Years ago, I really struggled with this type of delegation. **Why pay someone to do work I could do myself?**

And of course that question leads to the classic time arbitrage discussion of getting work done for a lower hourly rate so you can focus your time on higher value activities.

You already understand that argument, so I won't dwell on it here.

Still, it's a challenge (at least for me) and it might be helpful to categorize some of your tasks in this way.

The second type of delegation is MUCH harder.

If you don't know how to do the work you're asking your virtual assistant to do, *how will you explain it to them?*

How will you know if they're qualified?

How will you know if they're doing it right?

This is where I've run into trouble, especially when trying to outsource large-scale technical projects. Sure, I drew up the project specs as best I could, but could I *really* tell if my contractor knew the best way to deliver the work?

(I feel the same way when I take my car to the shop. "Sir, we inspected the vehicle and found your front drive shaft power steering discombobulator is worn out. I recommend replacing it immediately.")

OK, if you say so.

There are a couple ways around this.

The first is to **get a second or third or fourth opinion.** If you approach each VA or contractor or outsourcing company with the same goal or desired outcome, you can compare their proposed solutions apples to apples.

The ones who take the time to understand your problem and desired destination are probably the ones that will be best to work with long-term.

The other method is to **learn the process yourself first.** For example, if I want to delegate my social media marketing, I can take the time to learn the strategies and tactics, and develop the processes and the documentation around them.

Then I'm in a much better position to train a VA to take over those tasks, and can probably find someone more affordable than if I was hiring for the "strategy" portion as well.

The tradeoffs are time and money. The first method is faster but more expensive, while the second is slower but cheaper.

But there aren't any shortcuts, at least that I'm aware of.

Do your requirements focus on the tasks you know how to do but shouldn't be doing, or the tasks you don't know how to do? Or both?

How to Write the Perfect Virtual Assistant Job Description

The perfect VA job description is one that covers all your requirements AND shows some personality. We've all read through job listings that sound like they were written by a machine:

> *The ideal candidate has a master's degree in accounting and 3-5 years experience in corporate tax audits. We seek a team player with strong interpersonal skills... blah blah blah*

If that doesn't sound like a cool job to you, it probably won't sound like a cool job to your prospective hires either.

Here's what I posted when I was looking for new VA:

I'm looking for a dedicated virtual assistant for a (hopefully) long-term engagement. I envision this being a full-time position.

You are a super-savvy Internet user who loves Excel and gets more excited than anyone probably should when discussing spreadsheets. You know the best sites to gather information and are an organizational whiz. You are a quick learner and work well without constant supervision.

You find ways to make the routine and mundane exciting. You are a master of efficiency and a guru of productivity. You speak and write English well, and are available to work full-time for the foreseeable future, with at least a few hrs overlap with US Pacific time 7am-5pm. You're comfortable with social media and genuinely care about customers.

An interest in shoes and fashion is a plus, as is experience with AdWords. You'll be doing daily website maintenance and marketing for a growing shoe shopping website.

If this is you, please apply with your resume and references. I will review the applications and probably ask the strongest contenders to submit a few trial tasks before moving to interview stage.

There are several advantages of doing it this way.

First, by showing some personality in your ad, you can expect to get some personality in your responses.

By using some slang and idioms, you can gauge each respondent's grasp of your English.

If you give a hint as to what the VA will actually be working on, you can get more qualified responses. I got several applicants (all female) exclaiming how much they love shoes and how this sounded like a dream job.

And finally, when you give specific instructions, you can immediately weed out those who do not follow them. I asked for a resume and references, yet a few applicants neglected to include those in their reply.

Go ahead and craft your perfect help-wanted ad that lets your personality shine through. Next, I'll show you where to post it to get the most qualified applicants.

The Great Debate: VA Company or Freelancer?

When thinking of hiring a virtual assistant, you basically have two choices. You can find a freelance virtual assistant, or you can use one of several reputable VA companies.

Virtual assistant companies have an office full of professional assistants ready to help you with whatever tasks you need done. They typically charge a monthly fee that will vary upon the number of hours of work you'll need done. Several virtual assistant companies will offer a free trial period, which will help you get an idea both for how well their virtual assistant will perform, and how much you will use the service.

In most cases, you'll pay more when you use a third-party VA company than you would with a freelancer, because the company incurs overhead costs like payroll processing, office infrastructure, and administrative support that freelancers do not.

Still, when a full-time virtual assistant is in the $1000 a month ballpark, there is certainly something to be said for the additional **support and security** a VA firm offers. You get the benefit of a team of workers and their pooled knowledge and experience.

With a virtual assistant company, you get on-site management and back-up support if your VA is sick, quits, or just isn't working out. Of course, on the other side of things, your VA may have to spend some of their time filling in for their co-worker who is out sick.

With a freelance virtual assistant, you have the advantage of being able to specify your unique requirements in advance (although several VA companies allow you to do this as well). This means you can **hire the perfect worker** for your needs, not just the first available virtual assistant.

Since your VA will probably be working from their home, the **costs will generally be lower** because there is no company office space, overhead, or profit to account for.

I've found that freelancers are great for one-time projects or quick tasks that require a specific area of expertise, but there are many full- and part-time freelance virtual assistants out there with a wide range of skills as well.

My most recent full-time VA hire was a freelancer I found on Elance (since rebranded to Upwork.com), and I've been extremely happy with her. If she leaves, it's true I'll have to start from scratch with someone new, but I'd have to train my backup VA at the big company just the same.

The downside of hiring a freelance virtual assistant is that if things aren't working out, you may not have much recourse. In contrast, many VA companies have satisfaction guarantees or can reassign your work to a new virtual assistant better able to accomplish your tasks.

The following section on where to post your help wanted ad will focus primarily on freelance VAs. To work with a VA company, you can follow a similar procedure, by just submitting your requirements through their contact forms online.

For an up-to-date directory of virtual assistant companies, please visit VirtualAssistantAssistant.com. (Disclosure: this is my site.)

The Rise of Specialist Virtual Assistant Services

One interesting development in the outsourcing world is the rise of specialist virtual assistant companies.

To be sure, you can still find the big call-center type operations in India and elsewhere offering every service under the sun, but more and more recently I'm seeing new companies really niche down in their service offerings.

If you've gone through your job requirements and found an area of delegation opportunity around a specific skillset, there is a strong probability a company exists to serve that exact need.

For example, if you need support for your WordPress site, you can get that done by WP Curve for $79/month.

If you need help creating content for your site or for clients, Copywriter Today has you covered.

If you need help with graphic design, companies like Undullify and Design Pickle have affordable monthly plans offering "unlimited" design tasks.

For transcriptions, there's Rev.com. For bookkeeping, Bench.co. For social media, there's 99dollarsocial.com.

The greatest benefit to these types of companies is they have a clearly defined scope of work, and you know exactly what you're going to get. There's little (if any) virtual assistant training involved and you can hit the ground running very quickly.

You can sign up for one of these services at significant cost savings over hiring a dedicated freelance virtual assistant to provide the same specialized service, and you don't have to worry about keeping a VA busy enough to "get your money's worth" with work they may or may not be qualified to perform.

These services are best if you have a somewhat predictable ongoing need for the type of service they offer. If your demand for graphics, for example, is still spotty, hold off on the Undullify subscription and just go with the one-off freelance projects.

(The same is true for any ongoing VA hire.)

Where to Post Your Job

There are several different places you can post your virtual assistant job. I'll show you where to go to get the best results, in order of increasing difficulty.

Virtual Assistant Companies

The easiest way to get started is by sharing your requirements with 2 or 3 virtual assistant companies. I'm hesitant to recommend any specific company here because I can't predict what might happen with them in the future.

For example, Tim Ferris praised Ask Sunday in *The 4-Hour Work Week* in 2007, but in 2011 they shut down completely for 2 months, didn't respond to customers, and left a lot of paying clients in the dark. They've since reopened and are rebuilding their reputation. Similarly, in 2015, the well-regarded US-based VA company Zirtual abruptly announced they were ceasing operations. After a last minute acquisition, they resumed business later that week, but the instability understandably shook many of the assistants and their clients.

You can find some reputable and well-reviewed VA companies at VirtualAssistantAssistant.com. After you do your homework, submit your job description and see if they have anyone to fit your needs. Again, I recommend contacting 2 or 3 different firms so you can compare the responses you get back.

A Note on Geography

Not long ago, the entire outsourcing and virtual assistant industry was all about India. This has changed dramatically. Today, you will find virtual assistants and virtual assistant companies all around the globe.

I've had contact with VA companies in the United States, the UK, Australia, Central and South America, South Africa, Pakistan, China, and even Dubai.

But the undisputed leader in virtual assistants right now is the Philippines. The wages are very affordable, the English education is excellent, and the general culture is a better fit for Western business practices.

When choosing a VA company or freelancer, take geography into consideration. If you have time, it can be an interesting experiment to interview a few candidates from different locations, and will give you a better idea of any potential language barriers and cultural differences.

Freelance Sites

The next place you can post your job is on any one of the large global freelance sites. I've had success with Elance, but I have friends who swear by oDesk. Luckily, the debate between the two is now a moot point. These were the two largest freelance marketplaces, and in 2015 they actually merged to form Upwork.com. The platform has a good and transparent feedback system in place, and offers fraud protection and dispute resolution for employers.

You can post to the site (it's free) and get a broad range of applicants. If you want to cast a wider net, other options include Guru.com, Freelancer.com, and PeoplePerHour.com.

In any site you choose, just look for the "Post Your Job" option, and they will guide you through the process. Once you're finished, you'll probably start getting applications within minutes.

Job Boards

Job boards can be an excellent resource for finding virtual assistants. I'll share some of the most popular VA-specific boards in the US and abroad where you can post your job.

First, in the US, you can check out **Virtual Assistant Forums** (www.virtualassistantforums.com). As the name suggests, the site is geared toward VAs themselves, but has a submit job/request for proposal option where you can broadcast your opening to the site's membership. It is free to post.

The next option is **VAnetworking.com**, a similar community of freelance VAs, where you can submit your job request for free.

You might also consider **VirtualAssistantville.com** or my personal favorite, **HireMyMom.com**, where you can look for qualified work-from-home moms to be your VA!

Overseas, the largest job board is **OnlineJobs.ph**, which has more than 150,000 Filipino VAs looking for work.

The Proactive Search

On both the freelance sites and the job board sites mentioned above, you can *proactively* browse the profiles of available virtual assistants. In fact, many entrepreneurs prefer this method because you can **filter by qualifications, location, and salary expectations**.

OnlineJobs.ph is the leading site for this style of proactive search, due to the depth of their applicant pool and their powerful filtering tools. The most important filter? English language skills. If their English is strong, everything else can be taught.

OnlineJobs.ph charges $49 a month for access to their service, but it shouldn't take longer than that to find your VA. Plus, the cost really is negligible when you think of the long-term time and money savings your VA brings to your business.

What About Craigslist?

Yes, Craigslist is worldwide, and yes, you can post help wanted ads for free. You may have even heard some success stories of people going onto Craigslist and finding the perfect VA.

When posting to international Craigslist boards, you may find a diamond in the rough. But for me, it's not worth sorting through all the spammers and the scammers. At least on the other 3rd party platforms there are vetting processes and feedback mechanisms to protect employers.

In the US, it's a different story as Craigslist is actually one of the leading job search platforms. If you're looking for a part-time or full-time VA locally or somewhere in the States, Craigslist can be a good bet. (Though it can be a pain to post to a dozen different cities.)

Regardless of how your source your VA candidates, you now have some work to do to find which one is truly the right fit for you and your business.

How to Thin Out the Herd

This is where the hiring process really starts to get interesting. By now you probably have a dozen or more virtual assistant applicants. It's time to thin out the herd, and for this, you sometimes have to **be ruthless**.

Didn't include a personal reply? *Gone.*

Didn't follow directions? *Gone.*

Zero earnings history or feedback? *Gone.*

4 Page Resume for a $6/hr job? *Gone.*

Application says "strong English skills" but is filled with typos and misspellings? *Gone.*

You get the idea.

In my job post I specifically asked for a "super-savvy Internet user," so I had no qualms about immediately rejecting candidates who applied with a Hotmail email address.

Yes, that's a nerdy email address joke.

You'll probably notice you have some applications from individuals and some from big companies.

There are a couple things I've started to look for in the portfolios of the applicants.

The first is their "**tested skills**." On Upwork, there is an opportunity for contractors to add their skills to their portfolio.

The funny thing is, these skills can be tested or merely "self-rated." For the tested skills, it will show you the percentile in which the contractor scored. If someone claims to be a php expert for instance, but only scored in the 25% percentile, I would hesitate to hire that person.

And obviously I wouldn't give much weight at all to the self-rated skills. Of course everyone thinks they're great – they're trying to get hired!

The second area of the portfolio I've taken to looking at is the **feedback from previous clients**.

However, you should know that the feedback ratings shown are typically inflated. My insider tip would be check out the number of jobs completed, compared to the number of completed jobs with feedback left.

If the contractor has a ton of jobs where no clients left any feedback, that to me would be a red flag. Why? Like it or not, many customers still subscribe to the old tenet of "if you don't have anything nice to say, don't say anything at all."

I suggest narrowing down your list of applications until you have about 4 or 6 strong matches. These can be either freelancers or VA companies. In fact, for the next stage, Trial Tasks, it might be worthwhile to test both.

An Alternative: A Virtual Headhunter?

A virtual assistant is supposed to save you time, right? So why spend so much time on the hiring process?

There are several **virtual assistant recruiting services** designed to help you speed up your search and skip straight to the interview process.

The two most well-known ones are Chris Ducker's Virtual Staff Finder and Joel Nelson's Zen Virtual Assistants Finder. For a one-time fee of $495, they will source 3 qualified Filipino candidates for you.

Basically you share your job requirements and they scour the labor pool in the Philippines for skilled local workers. Then you interview them as you normally would and choose the best fit.

The advantage is the time saved in screening candidates and filtering all the noise from your job postings. You know you're getting pre-screened VAs because the company has a reputation to uphold.

After you make your selection, they work from home and you pay them directly (more on that later). The typical *full-time* salary might range from $400 to $750 depending on what skills you're looking for.

All in all, you'll spend a little more upfront to save yourself some time initially, and find a suitable VA for a great long-term wage.

It's kind of like outsourcing your outsourcing!

How to Ask for Trial Tasks

Now that you've narrowed down your list of applicants, it's time for a **performance test**. You wouldn't buy a car without taking it for a test drive first, right?

Ask each of your remaining candidates if they will be willing to work through an hour or two of trial tasks. Most will agree to this as long as your trial isn't outrageously long or complex.

Here's how to create your performance test. Do some work as you normally would, but as you're working, create a set of instructions for your candidates. I recommend 2 or 3 different tasks to see how they do in different areas.

For example, you might ask for:

- One online research task – Find 3 footwear wholesalers in California and send me their contact details.
- One spreadsheet task – Check inventory levels of this season's new shoes.

- One writing sample – Write 250-300 words on the inexplicable continued popularity of UGG boots.

If you anticipate your job involving customer service or phone skills, have a friend pretend to be an angry customer and see how they handle the situation.

Most recently, I also included instructions to contact me via skype if anything was unclear related to the trial tasks. I was surprised that most candidates preferred to feel their way through the tasks on their own – even if it meant missing the point entirely and not following the directions – rather than ask me for clarification. Only one VA contacted me via skype, and she got the job.

As a best practice, ask each virtual assistant candidate for the **same tasks**, so you can compare the results to the others and to your own work.

When judging the results, look for accuracy and attention to detail. Is this person someone who, with a little training, could be a valuable asset to your team?

These trial tasks will help you narrow down the field a little more before you move to your interviews.

How to Interview a Virtual Assistant

I think interviewing is an important step in hiring a virtual assistant. You're about to let someone into your life and your business, so it only makes sense to **get to know them** a little bit first.

You'll get a sense for how they speak. Are they confident? Shy? How is their English? How do they think, and how seriously are they taking this opportunity?

For a lot of people, this might be your first interview on the other side of the table. It's nice to be the one asking the questions, but it can be stressful too.

I suggest using skype to conduct your interviews. The call quality is generally pretty good, and if you and your candidate have webcams, you can even see each other during the call which is really helpful.

In fact, I think a video call for the interview is a must. So much communication is non-verbal. Being able to look a candidate in the eye and see their body language is a critical aspect of any interview.

The best interviews play out like a dialogue, rather than an interrogation. I like to give the candidate ample time to ask questions of their own, as well as give a little background about myself and my company.

You can find dozens of websites with sample interview questions, but here are some of my favorites. (Some may not apply directly to you, depending on the type of VA you're interviewing):

- Tell me about yourself. What's your background?
- Out of all the jobs on Upwork, what attracted you to this one?
- Of the sample tasks, which did you like best and why?
- How would you market this product/this website/this service?
- In your work history, what kind of work are you most proud of?
- If you have a question and I'm not available, what would you do?
- What keeps you motivated?

In their work history, one important thing I look for is experience working remotely or working from home. You'll also have to cover the basic housekeeping questions, like their available start-date and expected working hours.

I would try to keep the interview around 15-20 minutes. (You're not trying to hire a new chairman of the board!)

It's also important to **keep realistic expectations**. You're not hiring a rocket scientist or a smooth-talking salesperson, and in many cases your candidates will be answering your questions in a second language. Just try and get a gauge for who they are, their enthusiasm, and their ability to learn quickly and follow directions.

A general rule is to interview three candidates.

You're Hired!

Once you decide on the winning candidate, you can negotiate your terms. You can generally negotiate salary at this point, but don't take it too far. You don't want to start your relationship on bad terms, and remember, if you're going through a freelance site like Upwork, they typically take a 10% cut out of whatever you pay.

At the onset, let them know you'd like to bring them on board on a trial basis for 2 weeks. I've found this worthwhile to see how things work out in real life. They'll be eager to impress you to earn a long-term position.

After that, you can simply edit the terms of your agreement and continue working with your new virtual assistant!

A Final Word of Caution:

If using a freelance site, some candidates will try and sweet-talk you into hiring them *outside of the system.* They'll offer a slightly lower price because they can avoid paying the Upwork fee.

I know because I fell for it.

This gentleman seemed like a stand-up guy, a real professional, and I trusted him and hired him outside of Elance.

Turns out he was a real professional scam artist. He didn't deliver the results he promised, and wouldn't return my phone calls and emails. It was a terrible experience and cost me a few thousand dollars and a lot of headache.

And the worst part was I had no recourse. Even though I found him through Elance, I didn't qualify for any of their buyer protections because the job wasn't on their books.

So don't make my mistake: **Use the system and sleep easy**.

After a period of time you'll have built up some trust; then it's ok to move off the platform.

SECTION 3:

WORKING WITH YOUR VIRTUAL ASSISTANT

Welcome Package

The first thing to do after hiring a new virtual assistant is to put together a digital welcome package for them. I'm not talking about flowers or chocolates, but think of it more as a new employee orientation.

Your welcome package can include an overview of your business, your goals and objectives, and your general expectations for your new VA.

Conditions of Employment – Independent Contractor

This is a simple document that explains the legal nature of your relationship should anyone question it down the road. It explains that the VA is an independent contractor of your company and sets forth some of the expectations listed below.

Note: This is optional for freelance VAs, and not necessary for virtual assistant companies.

Non-Disclosure/Non-Compete

Asking your VA to sign a non-disclosure/non-compete agreement is optional but can be good for peace of mind. On the plus side, it gives the impression you've got your act together with some official-looking paperwork. You can find free templates for this type of agreement just by searching on Google.

Logins and Passwords

Your VA will likely need access to your systems, so you'll need to create new user accounts for them and include those in your welcome package.

Software

If their job will require any special software, make sure they are aware of that and have it loaded on their system. If the software is specific to your business I would suggest paying for their download and installation license, but of course you're welcome to negotiate that as well.

Working Hours

Depending on what time zone your VA is in, your working hours may not have a lot of overlap. If you don't require your VA to be in the office at the same time you are, it's not an issue, and there's no need for them to work the night shift if you're not going to need real-time communication.

Many virtual assistants enjoy the job because of the **flexible hours**, so try to be accommodating to their preferred schedule. As long as the work gets done it shouldn't be a problem, and you'll know right away if it is.

That said, you're the boss and you can ask them to work the hours that you need.

Pay Day

You've already agreed on a salary and terms, but this formalizes the agreement and lets your VA know when and how they'll be paid.

Communication

Include your preferred means of communication. Should your VA call you with any questions, find you on instant messenger, send you an email or text, or just use their best judgment and move on?

I would set up some guidelines on expected response times for emails or voicemails. I'm a stickler for communication, as there's nothing worse than lobbing emails into a black hole and never getting any reply. But aside from my experience with the terrible programmer who duped me into working with him outside the Elance system, I've never had an issue with poor communication.

Performance

How will you measure your VA's performance? If you have **specific metrics** you use to evaluate your business, share those with your VA. To the extent they can influence the results, I've found they're very eager to deliver value to their clients.

You may have heard Peter Drucker's old adage, "*What gets measured gets managed.*" It's completely true for working with virtual assistants too.

If you don't currently have any quantitative targets for your VA to shoot for, make some up. Some examples may include blog posts, backlinks, sales, leads, avg. response time, ads created, or Facebook fans – whatever jobs you can measure the results for.

Bonus Opportunities

This can be tied to the performance metrics above, but if you have any opportunities for your VA to earn extra money by **adding to your bottom line**, the welcome package is the perfect time to share them with your VA and get them even more excited about the job.

How to Train Your VA

Every hour you invest in training your virtual assistant will **pay off exponentially** down the road. For example, if you have a routine task that takes you half an hour a day, it might only take you an hour or two to train your VA to do the task and you won't have to worry about it again. That initial two-hour investment could end up saving you over 600 hours a year!

In that sense, training your VA delivers the most bang-for-your-buck of probably any activity.

Writing Clear Guidelines

If I'm getting back unsatisfactory work from a VA, it's usually **my fault**. Why?

My instructions must not have been clear enough.

Learning how to give **clear and detailed instructions** is definitely a challenge, but it's a worthwhile management exercise.

I remember this writing lesson from elementary school; we had to create a step-by-step guide to drawing a stick-figure for someone who had never drawn one before. Think about the level of detail required for that.

Draw a circle – How big? Where on the page? Color it in?

Draw a line coming out the bottom – Straight? Squiggly? How long?

And on and on ...

But it's the same way when working with a VA for the first time. When it comes to your business processes, they may not be all that different from the person who's never drawn a stick figure before.

For that reason, you can't be too detailed or specific when giving instructions in your systems and how you want things done.

Documentation

The benefit of writing all this down is now you'll have a record to refer to in the future. It's like creating a mini training manual you can use again and again, and documenting your processes forces you into a higher-level managerial role.

Your virtual assistant can add their own notes to these files if they discover their own best practices. Down the road, they may be the ones training your next VA!

You can also create video and audio tutorials that really pack a punch. Reading about how to do something is fine, but watching it happen is a surefire way to get the message across.

I like to get on a Skype call and use their screen sharing feature, but there are some other cool tools you can use too (more on that in just bit).

Daily Tasks

One thing that has worked well for me has been to set up a series of **routine daily tasks** for my VA to do. These were items that were eating up a lot of my time, and I don't have to worry about them anymore. My VA knows they are her responsibility and gets them done without any hesitation.

Basically you want to give your VA everything they need to be successful in their job and deliver results. It may take a little extra hand-holding in the beginning but it will pay off big down the road.

Daily Check-Ins

Some people like to get a daily check-in email from the VA, with a summary of what they accomplished that day and what they plan on working on tomorrow. Beyond that, they can include weekly and monthly goals as well.

It can also be a good idea for them to write down what problems they encountered and if they could use your help with anything.

The email is more for your VA to get into the habit of **focusing on the deliverables**, more than an excuse for you to get more email. After a while, you won't even have to read the email, but you'll know the work is getting done.

Would You Want to Work for You?

It's important your virtual assistant knows what you expect of them, and equally, what they can expect from you. For many people, their first VA is their first real management experience, and it can be a challenge.

Think of the **best boss** you ever had. What made them great? Your job now is to strive to be an equally great boss for your VA.

Micromanaging

Nobody likes to be micromanaged, and spending too much time and energy micromanaging your VA is counterproductive to your goals in hiring them in the first place. Their work is supposed to **free up your time**, not demand more of it.

Virtual assistants take pride in their work and want to keep their clients happy. I'm not suggesting you never check their work, but I would caution spending too much time on it.

Once or twice a week I'll do a small **quality control check** on my VA, and once or twice a month I'll do a more in-depth look at their work and decision making. But lately even this has been a waste of time as there really hasn't been anything major to take issue with.

When you find something wrong, use it as an opportunity for coaching and to update or clarify your instructions, rather than as reason for reprimand.

Challenging Work

If your virtual assistant is doing mundane, repetitive, mind-numbing work for you day after day, they're going to end up hating their job. No matter how happy they seem to be, no one can do data entry (for example) 8 hours a day without wanting to **gouge their eyes out**.

For this reason, it's a good idea to throw your VA some more challenging work every now and then for some variety. This could be brainstorming new marketing ideas, fielding customer questions, writing blog articles, or really anything outside their "normal" responsibilities.

I believe this creates an enjoyable work environment and **long-term loyalty**.

Growth Opportunities

Just like you, virtual assistants are looking to expand their skill sets and advance their careers. As your business grows, consider what additional opportunities there may be for your VA.

If you can give your VA extra responsibilities as time goes on, it will help foster a positive long-term relationship.

Praise and Bonuses

If you're happy with the work your virtual assistant is doing for you, **let them know**. Simple as that.

Flexibility

You probably don't need to set up any formal rules for vacation days or sick days. My experience has been that VAs are very hard-working and rarely ask for time off. Because of that, I have no problem at all when they do need to take some time away from work for whatever reason.

Should you pay for time off? It's totally up to you. It's not required or even expected, but it's a small gesture that generates huge returns in VA job satisfaction and loyalty. Obviously you can revisit your policy if it starts to get abused.

Feedback

I try to make a point to regularly ask my VA for feedback:

- How are you liking the job?
- Are there any projects you'd like to work on?
- What's the worst part about the job?
- What would you like to see from me as the boss?
- Is there anything you're having trouble with?

Tools of the Trade

Working with virtual assistants has never been easier, thanks to the many web-based tools we now have at our disposal. Of course this list barely scratches the surface, but highlights some of the most popular services as well as my favorites.

Skype

Skype is a free Internet calling and instant messaging platform. You can call other Skype users for free, or any number around the world for low per-minute rates.

I use Skype to interview my VAs, call and IM with them after they're hired, and share files on a daily basis. One of the best features of Skype is their free screen sharing so you can walk your VA through a specific process step-by-step while on the call with them.

One alternative is to use a Google+ hangout, which also allows live screen sharing for free.

Google Drive

Google Drive (formerly Google Docs) is Google's free online version of the familiar Microsoft Office software suite.

As a long-time Microsoft Office user, I was a late adopter when it came to Google Drive. The intuitive file sharing won me over; it allows for multiple users to have a file open and edit it in real time.

After years of emailing spreadsheets back and forth, I've finally come around to the power of Google Drive. I do miss some of my favorite Excel functions, but most of the time it works just fine.

Dropbox

Dropbox is a cloud-based file storage service. It is free for up to 2 GB of storage, and you can earn more free storage by referring your friends.

For sharing files outside Google Drive, I like to use Dropbox. I became a big fan of Dropbox after a recent hard drive failure wiped out all my saved data. Now I create automatic online backups of my important files.

You can give your VA password-protected access to the whole Dropbox or just certain folders.

Other Popular Tools

- Basecamp – Beautifully designed project management software. Many VA companies already use this to help manage their VA-client relationships.

- Slack – Teamwork platform designed to keep you out of your inbox.
- Google Calendar – Keep all your appointments in this free online system.
- Jing – Create free screen capture videos for training.
- Do.com – Slick task management platform.
- Open Office – Open source (free) version of Office software.
- LastPass – Secure password sharing software perfect for virtual teams.

Time Tracking and Work Monitoring

When working with a virtual assistant for the first time, employers often ask, "How do I know they are really working?"

Well, whether or not any work is getting done would be a hint. But beyond the obvious, **managing productivity** with remote workers is a big concern, and it's understandable why a greater level of oversight can be invaluable. There are a couple of different options to accomplish this goal.

Built-In Tracking

If you hire your VA through Upwork or certain other freelance marketplaces, work tracking mechanisms are automatically in place. Your virtual assistant logs in when they start their day and logs out when they are done. The system takes screen capture images of their system at random intervals so you can see what they're working on at any given time – or if they're off reading the news or browsing Facebook.

With the main freelance sites, logging into their tracking system is mandatory for the VA getting paid.

Tracking Software

For virtual assistants hired outside the Upwork ecosystem, you'll need some third-party tracking software if you want to closely monitor your VA's workday. There are several viable options that share similar features to the Upwork systems.

For example, HiveDesk is a project-management platform that stores timesheet data based on logins and takes random screenshots. Plans for 3 workers start at $15 per month.

Another popular option is Time Doctor. This robust software tracks work time, blocks productivity-killing websites, takes random screen captures, and more. There is a monthly fee that varies based on the number of users.

My Way

After the first few days, I found that I never looked at the screenshots Elance was taking. It's a nice feature to have if performance ever slips, but I think my time is better spent **managing for results** rather than babysitting my VA.

And so what if the screenshots turned up a Facebook page every now and then? I'm not sure it's realistic for someone to work an 8 hour shift without ever taking a break. I know I couldn't do it, so why should I expect the same from a virtual assistant? **They're real people, not machines**.

Now if you begin to notice a pattern and productivity was suffering, you would need to take action.

I currently don't use any tracking software – the only "system" in place is the instruction to login to Skype first thing in the morning and to use a Google Drive timesheet to keep track of the hours worked each day. But even that is pretty much on the **honor system**.

Once you have a decent track record of results and performance expectations, you no longer have to worry about time/screenshot tracking.

I think you'll be surprised by the reliability of your VA. One day I came online and didn't see my VA on Skype, which was literally unheard of. After a momentary panic that she might have quit without telling me, I got a text from her boyfriend's cell phone explaining she was trying to get online but a massive storm had caused an Internet and power outage in their town!

How to Pay Your Virtual Assistant

Of course your virtual assistant is eventually going to want to get paid for all the great work they're doing!

Virtual Assistant Company

If you're working with a virtual assistant company, they make this very easy. Payment is typically made monthly via **PayPal or by credit card**. The company will probably set up recurring billing so you don't even have to worry about it.

When it comes to cancellation, you generally just have to give notice before the next billing cycle.

Upwork Virtual Assistant

With an Upwork virtual assistant, payment is handled weekly through PayPal or credit card based on the number of hours logged into their system.

Freelance Virtual Assistant

For freelance VAs, you're free to negotiate your own payment schedule and terms. I prefer to pay monthly because it means less accounting, but many VAs prefer a more frequent payment schedule. It's totally between you and your VA to decide; there's no standard that I'm aware of.

I pay through PayPal because it seems to be the **universally accepted standard**. The fees are lower if you choose to draw from a bank account rather than a credit card.

Another popular option is Xoom. They specialize in low-fee international payments. Xoom is sometimes preferred by Filipinos over PayPal (though now the company is owned by PayPal).

A new money transfer service from the team at OnlineJobs.ph called EasyPay aims to provide a reliable method for paying virtual assistants in the Philippines. At press time, they are in a private beta.

For US-freelancers, you can still use PayPal, set up direct deposit, or use a funds transfer system supported by your bank, such as Chase QuickPay.

It is common for the employer to pass whatever transfer fee is charged onto the VA, but that is something you could split with them or discuss in advance how it will be handled.

Regardless of how you choose to pay your virtual assistant, the most important consideration is to **be timely with your payments**. This will go a long way toward strengthening your relationship.

To make life easier, you can have your VA send you an invoice each pay period so you have documentation for your accounting and a reminder to make the payment.

One Cautionary Tale

With virtual assistant companies, it is standard to pre-pay for the service. For example you might be billed on July 1st for work to be completed in July. That's fine and totally normal.

However, with freelance virtual assistants, **don't pre-pay**. While it's rare to hear stories of people paying upfront and then having their VA flake on them, there's no reason to risk it. If your VA is requesting advance payment right out of the gate, that could be a bad sign. Perhaps you can suggest an initial weekly payment schedule instead.

That way both parties can build trust and minimize their exposure. Keep in mind that from their perspective, working a full month before getting paid is a big risk if YOU flake.

BONUS SECTION:

THE 7 HABITS OF HIGHLY EFFECTIVE OUTSOURCERS

The 7 Habits of Highly Effective Outsourcers

Outsourcing and delegation are skills like any others. They can be learned and improved with practice.

No one is an instant expert, and those who claim to be are full of it.

But there are specific actions you can take to be a more effective outsourcer, and I want to share those now. With apologies to Stephen Covey, these 7 habits mirror those found in his classic self-help book.

Habit 1: Be Proactive

This is the most obvious of the habits and the good news is you're already being proactive by reading this book!

For me, one of the most stressful parts of being an entrepreneur is not having a boss to give me direction. Now don't get me wrong, most of the time I love it, but the independence necessitates a higher level of self-initiative.

You have to take control of your business and your life all on your own; no one else will do it for you.

When it came to a hiring a virtual assistant for the first time, I knew I needed help but didn't know where to turn. Instead of taking action quickly, I spent a ton of time analyzing all my options.

I thought I was being proactive. I thought the perfect solution would fall into my lap, or that my workload would somehow alleviate itself.

Of course it didn't work that way.

In outsourcing, here are some specific, proactive steps you can take to streamline the process:

- Track your time to discover areas of opportunity; activities or tasks that could be handled by someone else.
- Create a detailed process manual for those tasks. The process manual is a document with step-by-step instructions anyone should be able to follow after minimal training.
- Create a detailed job description or work spec.

Being proactive is about being able to act quickly when business growth or another factor dictates the need for additional help.

Even if you're not ready to hire a virtual assistant now, you'll eventually get to that point and the work you do in preparation will help make the hiring process that much easier.

After the hire, your job shifts to one of proactive communication and engagement. A proactive manager will assign tasks promptly and efficiently, solicit feedback on an ongoing basis, and anticipate the needs of their VA in advance.

For many people, working with a virtual assistant is their first time in a "management" role. You have to take control of the relationship to make sure it is a positive experience for both parties.

A proactive approach puts you in the driver's seat and keeps you there throughout the outsourcing engagement.

It also means taking responsibility when things don't go according to plan (as they sometimes don't!) and getting back on that horse when the time comes.

Habit 2: Begin with the End in Mind

I find it helpful to visualize my ideal scenario at the onset of any project. I write down my goals and how I picture the results.

For example, when it comes to hiring a virtual assistant, your ideal scenario might be never having to do data entry work and having the evenings free to spend with your family.

There a couple ways to do this.

The first is to create a personal or business **"mission statement"** if you don't have one already.

Your mission statement doesn't have to any drawn-out corporate mumbo-jumbo. It can be a very simple one-sentence vision of where you want to be.

Here are a few examples of mission statements that begin with the end in mind:

- I am a best-selling author.
- We are the #1 provider of _____.

- I never work weekends.
- We are a $1 million company.

In each case, the mission statement paints a picture of the end goal, and in doing so, helps dictate the work necessary to reach that goal.

It's like picking your destination on the map. Only after you do that can you effectively chart your path to get there.

Another way of beginning with the end in mind is dreamlining, popularized by Tim Ferriss in *The Four Hour Workweek*.

Dreamlining is similar to crafting a mission statement, but gets more specific. It focuses on 3 areas:

1. Having
2. Being
3. Doing

The first item, Having, can relate to material possessions (or lack thereof). For instance, having a nice house in a nice neighborhood is a common dreamline item.

Being can be flexible as well. Being fluent in Spanish, being self-employed, or being a ski bum are all perfectly acceptable dreamline goals.

Finally, Doing is related to how you'll spend your time on a day-to-day basis. It could be writing, running a restaurant, racing motorcycles, or really anything you want to do!

The end result is a dreamline statement that might look like this: "I'll have nothing more than I can fit in a backpack, be taking amazing travel photos and selling them online, while visiting the world's most beautiful locations."

In either case, beginning with the end in mind is just a fancy way of setting goals. It's a way to put into words what hiring a virtual assistant will mean for your business and your life.

When it comes to outsourcing, you have to have a picture of what success looks like. Consider this habit a measuring stick. Without it, it's impossible to judge how effective your outsourcing efforts are.

Habit 3: Put First Things First

This habit is the essence of what outsourcing allows you to do. By delegating the jobs that others can do, you can focus on your high-value activities.

When you start tracking your time, you'll learn how many hours you spend on your most important tasks, and also how much time you spend on everything else. It will help you identify which tasks only you can do, and which can be offloaded.

Similarly, you may find that a minority of your efforts produce the majority of the results (whether that be income, enjoyment, or both).

Putting first things first is the 80/20 rule in practice.

The most effective outsourcers have a clear picture of the work they need and love to do, which allows them to prioritize their schedules and delegate the non-essential tasks.

In larger businesses, you may hear about **"focusing on your core competencies**." I believe this is another way of expressing the habit of putting first things first.

If an activity is not essential to your business surviving and thriving, why not let someone else do it (or eliminate it entirely)? That way you can focus solely on what you do better than anyone else in the world.

Habit 4: Think Win-Win

A mutually beneficial relationship is critical to the long term success of your outsourcing arrangement.

The "win" for you is obvious and has been covered at length: cost savings, time freed up, improved productivity.

But a "win" for your virtual assistant or outsourcing partner is equally important. If the relationship is too one-sided, they won't stick around.

So what constitutes a win for a virtual assistant?

- Consistent employment
- Source of income to supplement or support family
- Opportunity to learn new skills
- Challenging and engaging work
- Autonomy and flexibility
- Performance bonuses
- Letters of reference to build a bigger client base

There might be a temptation to drive your rates to the lowest possible prices, negotiate strict contract penalties, and otherwise be a hard-ass boss, but I would caution against that. When you approach outsourcing with a win-win mentality, you have far better odds of success.

Just like any business transaction, a great outsourcing relationship starts with creating value for both parties involved. And as the outsourcer, it's on you to initiate and communicate that win-win mindset.

Habit 5: Seek First to Understand, Then to be Understood

Remember the old saying, "You have 2 ears and one mouth. Use them accordingly."? It means take the time to listen before trying to get your point across.

At the onset of your outsourcing journey, understanding the processes and best practices can save you hours of time and literally thousands of dollars of poorly allocated budget.

During the interview process, listening – really listening – is far more important than worrying about what your next question is going to be.

If you're hiring someone overseas or from a different culture than yours, it is especially crucial to invest some time in learning about their business customs and practices. For example, some cultures seem to consider asking clarifying questions as a sign of ignorance or stupidity. But when starting a new job, everyone has questions!

Taking the time to understand some of these potential cultural quirks can save confusion and headache down the road.

By listening to the questions your virtual assistant asks, you'll be able to refine your process manuals and instructions to make more sense and yield better results. On top of that, they may share a new way of doing things or a new way to solve a problem you hadn't thought of before.

It could be a really great new idea, but if you're too busy barking out orders you'll miss it for sure.

Your virtual assistant will know their voice is being heard and that you care about what they have to say. And it goes both ways. By showing you can be a good listener, they are more likely to behave similarly when it's your turn to give direction.

Habit 6: Synergize

Synergy is often described as how a team working together can make 1 and 1 equal 3. Indeed, you and your outsourcing partners should be able to create a result greater than the sum of your parts.

Effective outsourcers maximize the strengths of all parts of their team, which creates a natural efficiency.

It sounds a little cliché, but you and your virtual assistant should complement each other, to achieve results together you couldn't have alone.

A good example of organizational synergy is with outsourced bookkeeping or accounting. Often the entrepreneur hates the prospect of managing the books, filing tax forms, or trying to navigate the latest rules and regulations. Meanwhile, the accountant loves the challenge of managing cash flows and maximizing deductions.

By outsourcing the accounting-related tasks, the entrepreneur can tap into this new synergy. He'll save his time to work on higher-value projects he enjoys, and the accountant may actually save him money by finding new deductions and opportunities to save on taxes.

Synergies grow and evolve over time, which means a long-term relationship is a key to this habit.

Habit 7: Sharpen the Saw

The Sharpen the Saw habit comes from a parable about a lumberjack who is busy chopping down trees. Eventually the blade of his saw gets dull and ineffective, but he keeps hacking away.

The point of the story is how important it is to step away (seemingly a step backward – I have trees to chop!), to take time to review your tools and resources.

The lumberjack loses a bit of time in sharpening his saw, but when he goes back to work he finds he is twice as efficient.

In outsourcing, we can "sharpen the saw" too. Make a point to step back and evaluate your outsourcing relationships periodically. Initially I would suggest doing this on a monthly basis, and then perhaps on a quarterly or semi-annual basis later on.

The idea is to take a moment to analyze what's working well, what's not, and what you may be able to do to improve upon your outsourcing results. Occasionally, it can be helpful to ask for an outside perspective as well.

You'll get objective feedback and be able to dive back in with fresh ideas and a renewed vigor.

As it relates to outsourcing, sharpening the saw might mean reviewing your process manuals or fine-tuning certain aspects of your business.

This final habit is a crucial element to long term success because the world never stands still for long. If you don't take time to recharge, review, and adapt, you might soon find yourself left behind; attacking tough new challenges with a dull blade.

WHAT'S NEXT?

Exclusive Free Bonus Offer!

As a special "thank you" for reading all the way to the end, I'd like to offer a **free 15-minute one-on-one strategy-session** with me via Skype to answer any questions you have about the material in this book or on outsourcing in general.

No sales pitch, no strings attached.

Use this link to schedule a time that works for you: http://meetme.so/NickLoper

Or if that's a little too up-close-and-personal, you can always send me an email at: nick@virtualassistantassistant.com.

I'd love to hear from you!

Thank you so much for reading!

Now that you know it all, the only thing left is to jump right in!

If you found the information helpful, please leave a quick review at Amazon. It's a huge help!

Thank you!

RESOURCES AND READING

Books

The One Minute Manager – Excellent read for first-time managers.

The 4-Hour Work Week – Great advice from Tim Ferriss on the 80/20 principle and working with VAs.

Virtual Freedom – Chris Ducker's guide to outsourcing and working with virtual staff.

The Virtual Assistant Solution – Michael Hyatt's guide to dealing with overwhelm and getting started with remote delegation.

The E-Myth Revisited – A powerful reminder to work ON your business rather than IN it.

Where to Find a VA

GoButler (www.gobutlernow.com) – Free text-message based VA service.

Fancy Hands (www.fancyhands.com) – US-based task assistance service.

MyTasker (www.mytasker.com) – Dedicated VA service in India.

OkayRelax (www.okayrelax.com) – Affordable dedicated assistance sold in task-based packages.

Efficise (www.efficise.com) – Popular task-based VA service in Pakistan.

Codeable (www.codeable.io) – Marketplace for WordPress developers.

Upwork (www.upwork.com) – Leading freelance marketplace.

Fiverr (www.fiverr.com) – Fun marketplace of goods and services starting at $5.

WP Curve (wpcurve.com) – Unlimited WordPress support sold as a monthly subscription.

Copywriter Today (www.copywritertoday.net) – Unlimited article writing service sold as a monthly subscription. Mention referral code VAA50 for half off your membership for life.

Undullify (www.undullify.com) – Unlimited graphic design tasks sold as a monthly subscription.

Rev (www.rev.com) – Audio and video transcription service for $1/minute.

Bench (bench.co) – Monthly bookkeeping service.

HireMyMom (www.hiremymom.com) – Search for a qualified work from home mom to be your VA.

OnlineJobs.ph (onlinejobs.ph) – Job board for Filipino VAs.

VAnetworking (www.vanetworking.com) – "The Social Network for Virtual Assistants." Great place to post a job.

Virtual Assistant Forums
(www.virtualassistantforums.com) – A gathering place
for freelance VAs where you can submit your jobs.

Virtual Assistantville (www.virtualassistantville.com) – A
directory and community of VAs to which you can
submit your job.

Virtual Staff Finder (www.virtualstafffinder.com) –
Virtual headhunting service in the Philippines.

Zen Virtual Assistants Finder
(zenvirtualassistantsfinder.com/vaa) – Filipino VA
recruiting service.

Virtual Assistant Education

Virtual Assistants 101 (www.chrisducker.com/virtual-
assistants-101/) – Tons of great content on working
with virtual assistants.

Virtual Assistant Assistant
(www.virtualassistantassistant.com) – Directory of
virtual assistant companies with honest user reviews.
Disclosure: this is my site.

Online Tools

Basecamp (www.basecamp.com) – Popular project-
management software.

Dropbox (www.dropbox.com) – Free online backup and
file storage.

HiveDesk (www.hivedesk.com) – Project-management
and time-tracking software for remote workers.

Jing (www.techsmith.com/jing.html) – Create screen capture videos to share.

LastPass (www.lastpass.com) – Secure password sharing software for virtual teams.

Payments.ph (www.payments.ph) – Pay Filipino VAs.

PayPal (www.paypal.com) – Send money online.

Skype (www.skype.com) – Free voice calls and IMs.

Slack (slack.com) – Team communication platform.

Time Doctor (www.timedoctor.com) – Monitor remote employees.

Xoom (www.xoom.com) – Pay your VAs anywhere in the world.

NOTES

The author's essay, "Is Outsourcing a Dirty Word?" first appeared on noobpreneur.com in May 2012.

Outsourcing in Action

This book was copyedited by a freelance editor found on Elance.com.

The cover was created by a graphic designer on Fiverr.com.

ABOUT THE AUTHOR

Nick Loper has been working with virtual assistants since 2005. The author and entrepreneur lives in Northern California with his wife Bryn, son Max, and a lovable giant Shih-Tzu called Mochi.

On a typical day you can find him working and walking on his treadmill desk, rooting for the Mariners, or skiing the Sierra pow.

He is the founder of VirtualAssistantAssistant.com.

If you found the information helpful, please leave a quick review at Amazon. It's a huge help!

Thank you!

ALSO BY NICK

The Side Hustle Path: 10 Proven Ways to Make Money Outside of Your Day Job

The Side Hustle Path Volume 2: 10 Proven Ways to Make Money Outside of Your Day Job

The Side Hustle Path Volume 3: 10 Proven Ways to Make Money Outside of Your Day Job

The Side Hustle Path Volume 4: 10 Proven Ways to Make Money Outside of Your Day Job

Treadmill Desk Revolution: The Easy Way to Lose Up to 50 Pounds in a Year – Without Dieting

The Small Business Website Checklist: A 51-Point Guide to Build Your Online Presence the Smart Way

Work Smarter: 500+ Online Resources Today's Top Entrepreneurs Use to Increase Productivity and Achieve Their Goals

Made in the USA
San Bernardino, CA
31 March 2016